# FENCING

## Training Journal

ISBN 978-1-944086-00-8

# My Goals

It's important to have goals to work for when you are a fencer. Fencing's hard work and it takes time to become better. You may get discouraged at times. If you do, you should look at your goals to get yourself motivated again.

Goals can be very small that you can accomplish this week. They may also be very big, and take years to get to. It's best to have a mix of smaller and larger goals. Small goals are good because they give you a burst of energy every time you achieve one. Larger goals are good because they give you something to work for that keeps you going for a long time.

**Small goals examples:** Learn a new attack; practice my parry 4 and parry 6 100 times a day for a week; practice footwork for 20 minutes three times this week.

**Larger goals examples:** score more touches against my most difficult opponent by the end of the month; receive fewer touches in my practice bouts; participate in one tournament each month for the next 4 months.

# My Goals

# My Goals

# My Goals

# My Goals

# My Goals

# My Goals

# My Goals

# My Goals

# Today's Activities and Achievements

# Today's Activities and Achievements

# Today's Activities and Achievements

# Today's Activities and Achievements

# Today's Activities and Achievements

# Today's Activities and Achievements

# Today's Activities and Achievements

# Today's Activities and Achievements

# Today's Activities and Achievements

# Today's Activities and Achievements

# Today's Activities and Achievements

# Today's Activities and Achievements

# Today's Activities and Achievements

# Today's Activities and Achievements

# Today's Activities and Achievements

# Today's Activities and Achievements

# Today's Activities and Achievements

# Today's Activities and Achievements

# Today's Activities and Achievements

# Today's Activities and Achievements

# Today's Activities and Achievements

# Today's Activities and Achievements

# Today's Activities and Achievements

# Today's Activities and Achievements

# Today's Activities and Achievements

# Today's Activities and Achievements

# Today's Activities and Achievements

# Today's Activities and Achievements

# Today's Activities and Achievements

# Today's Activities and Achievements

# Today's Activities and Achievements

# Today's Activities and Achievements

# Today's Activities and Achievements

# Today's Activities and Achievements

# Today's Activities and Achievements

# Today's Activities and Achievements

# Today's Activities and Achievements

# Today's Activities and Achievements

# Today's Activities and Achievements

# Today's Activities and Achievements

# Today's Activities and Achievements

# Today's Activities and Achievements

# Today's Activities and Achievements

# Today's Activities and Achievements

# Today's Activities and Achievements

# Today's Activities and Achievements

# Today's Activities and Achievements

# Today's Activities and Achievements

# Today's Activities and Achievements

# Today's Activities and Achievements

# Today's Activities and Achievements

# Today's Activities and Achievements

# Today's Activities and Achievements

# Today's Activities and Achievements

# Today's Activities and Achievements

# Today's Activities and Achievements

# Today's Activities and Achievements

# Today's Activities and Achievements

# Today's Activities and Achievements

# Today's Activities and Achievements

# Today's Activities and Achievements

# Today's Activities and Achievements

# Today's Activities and Achievements

# Today's Activities and Achievements

# Today's Activities and Achievements

# Today's Activities and Achievements

# Today's Activities and Achievements

# Today's Activities and Achievements

# Today's Activities and Achievements

# Today's Activities and Achievements

# Today's Activities and Achievements

# Today's Activities and Achievements

# Today's Activities and Achievements

# Today's Activities and Achievements

# Today's Activities and Achievements

# Today's Activities and Achievements

# Today's Activities and Achievements

# Today's Activities and Achievements

# Today's Activities and Achievements

# Today's Activities and Achievements

# Today's Activities and Achievements

# Today's Activities and Achievements

# Today's Activities and Achievements

# Today's Activities and Achievements

# Today's Activities and Achievements

# Today's Activities and Achievements

# Today's Activities and Achievements

# Today's Activities and Achievements

# Today's Activities and Achievements

# Today's Activities and Achievements

# Today's Activities and Achievements

# Today's Activities and Achievements

# Today's Activities and Achievements

# Today's Activities and Achievements

# Today's Activities and Achievements

# Today's Activities and Achievements

# Today's Activities and Achievements

# Today's Activities and Achievements

# Today's Activities and Achievements

# Today's Activities and Achievements

# Today's Activities and Achievements

# Today's Activities and Achievements

# Today's Activities and Achievements

# Today's Activities and Achievements

# *Today's Activities and Achievements*

# Today's Activities and Achievements

# Today's Activities and Achievements

# Today's Activities and Achievements

# Today's Activities and Achievements

# Today's Activities and Achievements

# Today's Activities and Achievements

# Today's Activities and Achievements

# Today's Activities and Achievements

# Today's Activities and Achievements

# Today's Activities and Achievements

# Today's Activities and Achievements

# Today's Activities and Achievements

# Today's Activities and Achievements

# Today's Activities and Achievements

# Today's Activities and Achievements

# Today's Activities and Achievements

# Today's Activities and Achievements

# Today's Activities and Achievements

# Today's Activities and Achievements

# *Today's Activities and Achievements*

# Today's Activities and Achievements

# Today's Activities and Achievements

# Today's Activities and Achievements

# Today's Activities and Achievements

# Today's Activities and Achievements

# Today's Activities and Achievements

# Today's Activities and Achievements

# Today's Activities and Achievements

# Today's Activities and Achievements

# Today's Activities and Achievements

# Today's Activities and Achievements

# Today's Activities and Achievements

# Today's Activities and Achievements

# Today's Activities and Achievements

# Today's Activities and Achievements

# Today's Activities and Achievements

# Today's Activities and Achievements

# Today's Activities and Achievements

# Today's Activities and Achievements

# Today's Activities and Achievements

# Today's Activities and Achievements

# Today's Activities and Achievements

# Today's Activities and Achievements

# Today's Activities and Achievements

# Today's Activities and Achievements

# Today's Activities and Achievements

# Today's Activities and Achievements

# Today's Activities and Achievements

# Today's Activities and Achievements

# Today's Activities and Achievements

# Today's Activities and Achievements

# Today's Activities and Achievements

# Today's Activities and Achievements

# Today's Activities and Achievements

# *Today's Activities and Achievements*

# Today's Activities and Achievements

# Today's Activities and Achievements

# Today's Activities and Achievements

# Today's Activities and Achievements

# Today's Activities and Achievements

# Today's Activities and Achievements

# Today's Activities and Achievements

# Today's Activities and Achievements

# Today's Activities and Achievements

# Today's Activities and Achievements

# Today's Activities and Achievements

# Today's Activities and Achievements

# Today's Activities and Achievements

# Today's Activities and Achievements

# Today's Activities and Achievements

# Today's Activities and Achievements

# Today's Activities and Achievements

# Today's Activities and Achievements

# Today's Activities and Achievements

www.ingramcontent.com/pod-product-compliance
Lightning Source LLC
Chambersburg PA
CBHW081348080526
44588CB00016B/2411
* 9 7 8 1 9 4 4 0 8 6 0 0 8 *